LAUGHTER.in the WALLS

LAUGHTER in the WALLS

Bob Benson

impact
books

Nashville, Tennessee

Contents

to those who put it there

I

LAUGHTER IN THE WALLS

Laughter In The Walls

I pass a lot of houses on my way home—
  some pretty,
    some expensive,
      some inviting—
but my heart always skips a beat
  when I turn down the road
and see my house nestled against the hill.
  I guess I'm especially proud
of the house and the way it looks because
  I drew the plans myself.
It started out large enough for us—
  I even had a study—
two teenaged boys now reside in there.
  And it had a guest room—
my girl and nine dolls are permanent guests.
  It had a small room Peg
had hoped would be her sewing room—
  the two boys swinging on the dutch door
have claimed this room as their own.

So it really doesn't look right now
as if I'm much of an architect.
    But it will get larger again—
one by one they will go away
        to work,
            to college,
        to service,
        to their own houses,
and then there will be room—
    a guest room,
    a study,
    and a sewing room
    for just the two of us.
But it won't be empty—
    every corner
        every room
    every nick
        in the coffee table
will be crowded with memories.
Memories of picnics,
        parties, Christmases,
    bedside vigils, summers,
        fires, winters, going barefoot,
    leaving for vacation, cats,
        conversations, black eyes,
    graduations, first dates,
        ball games, arguments,
    washing dishes, bicycles,
        dogs, boat rides,
    getting home from vacation,
        meals, rabbits and
    a thousand other things
        that fill the lives
    of those who would raise five.
    And Peg and I will sit
quietly by the fire
    and listen to the
        laughter in the walls.

Tardiness

You were late
    but I wasn't alarmed
because you are always late.
    I can't exactly remember if
you made the wedding on time
    but if per chance
        you did come down
            the aisle promptly
it was one of the last times.

        You said you'd meet me
at seven and we'd have dinner—
    just the two of us
so I laid out enough work
    to last until seven-thirty.
        Seven came—
        but you didn't,
            seven-thirty showed—
        but you hadn't.
The clock said seven forty-five
    but the empty street below
        said you hadn't arrived
    and I found myself
leaning back in my chair
    with the work pushed aside
looking up the street
    for the station wagon
    and you.

Surprising how much of one's life
    can go by in a few minutes—
flashbacks of meetings we have had
    after work, for lunch,
        home from traveling,
            after an hour,
            after a day,
            after a week,
                but everytime
with the same little quickness
    in my throat that I felt
as I waited for you now
        for dinner.

You came and we ate,
    laughed and talked
        and went home.
And you, who probably know me
    better than anyone
        else in the world
didn't even suspect
        what it meant to me
    to see you coming
        down the street
            at seven forty-seven.

Trophys And Tarnish

You've had a good year, Bob—
   a starting position,
     a trip to the regionals,
trophys, medals, honors,
     recognition from your
friends and teachers.
It was an impressive list of
     accomplishments for
a sixteen year old—
and they were won in
     open competition—
       at a price
     in toil, study and sweat.
But trophys tarnish
     and honors fade.
Already a soph has his eye
   on a jersey number thirty-four
and some kid has made up

his mind to push you
further back in the class.
   Sooner or later someone
will score more baskets,
   and do better than you've done.
So really the important thing
   is not the deed well done
   or the medal that you possess
but the dedication and dreams
   out of which they grow.
You must have a left handed layup,
      a behind-the-back pass,
   a high percentage from the line
      and a fall away jumper,
but you must always have
   words that stir the imagination,
thoughts which haunt your mind
   and dreams which fill your heart
for out of dreams—deeds grow.

He Said His Lines

One of our sons, Mike,
    wanted to take private speech—
he's such a talker anyway,
    I recommended "hush" instead.
But it was inexpensive,
        and he was interested
        so we let him.

The climax of the year's labor
        was a two-hour long
        assortment of
            clowns,
                kings,
                    rabbits,
                and forgotten lines
known as the Speech Recital
    given to a devoted audience
        of eager parents
            and trapped friends.
Mike was a king.
    He looked rather regal too,
    if I do say so myself.
At least until the queen,
    a head taller and
    twenty pounds heavier,
stood beside him casting a pall
    on his regality.
He had only three lines to say—
    nine months of speech,
    three short lines—
and they came very very late,
    in the last moment
        of the last act
            of the very last play.
Anyway you looked at it
    he was not the star—
at least to anyone except a couple
    about halfway back on the left side.

It was a long evening
    and it was miserably hot
but Mike waited
    and he was ready
and he said his lines
    and he said them well.
Not too soon, not too late,
    not too loud, not too soft,
but just right
    he said his lines.

I'm just a bit player, too,
    not a star in any way—
but God gave me a line or so
    in the pageant of life,
and when the curtain falls
    and the drama ends—
    and the stage is vacant at last—
I don't ask for a critic's raves
    or fame in any amount.
I only hope that He can say,
    "He said his lines,
Not too soon, not too late,
    not too loud, not too soft,
He said his lines
    and he said them well."

Remember you can be a
bit player in God's
pageant --- you were
chosen --- Be ready ē your
lines + don't worry if the
show's a success.

23

I Never Took A Step

It was Pioneer Day,
　　Hendersonville's answer to
　　the Rose Parade,
　　the all-star game,
　　the World's Fair,
　　and the Mardi Gras—
all rolled into one
colorful but tiring day.
Between helping with fish fry,
　　Peg's aid in the cake sale,
　　boys in the all-star games,
　　Mike in different costumes
　　for parade and pageant,
　　it was a very busy day.

I was on the sidewalk,
　　camera ready and focused
　　for Mike who would come
　　clowning down the street.
I waited through bands,
　　army tanks, ponies—
　　majorettes, floats
　　but no sign of Mike.

So I waited through motorcycles,
     drill teams, Indians,
     stray dogs and a dozen other clowns,
but still no Mike.
I finally found Mike
   at the parade's dispersal—
   his face a combination of
   freckles, grease paint,
   perspiration—and shame.
"I chickened out," he said.
   "How far did you ride?"
"I never took a step."

Suddenly I remembered days
   I'd started out with high
resolve to carry the Master's
   banner in the procession of
   life—
And nights that found me
   defeated, discouraged,
   ashamed—knowing that
   I'd never taken
     a step for Him.

And remembering the flood of
   compassion, mercy, kindness
   and grace which He gave,
     I said to Mike,
   "There will be other days
   and other parades. You're
   still the finest clown I know."
Mike's face burst into smiles
   my heart burst into song,
And for just a moment I knew
   the joy of Christlikeness.

The Big News

The newspaper headlines
    screamed the news—
big, bold, black, front page—
    SHEPARD SUCCESSFUL IN
VAULT INTO SPACE.
But the real news,
    the big, big story
was tucked away neatly
    on the bottom corner of page seven.
BENSON: Mr. and Mrs. Robert G.,
111 Haven Street, Hendersonville,
Lori Leigh, born May 2nd,
Baptist Hospital.

There's nothing so important
    about her, you say.
Well, she thinks there is—
She has completely
    rescheduled the family,
        taken over the den,
    claimed a refrigerator shelf.

I think she's important too—
important because she's mine—
mine to love—
    tiny fingers,
        dimpled chin,
            shining eyes.
Mine to care for—
    food and thoughts,
        clothes and faith,
            school and habits.
She's plenty important to me.

She's important to God, too—
important because she's His.
Yes, Lori Leigh and
    Kathi Ann,
        James Alan,
            Terri Leah,
and all of the seventeen
    new folk in the cradleroll.
For people are more important
    to God
        than accomplishments.
What does he care about
    moonshots,
        world championships,
            space rides?
These are just
    deeds to be outdone,
        records to be broken,
    events to be overshadowed.
But these little folk will
dwell with Him forever.

The big story is not always
    on the front page.
    The real news—
        the big stories—
    are about people—
people like Lori Leigh.

Instant Obedience

There are three ways
    to get to our dining room—
    up from the living room,
        thru the hall,
    or in from the kitchen.
The conventional route to
    the breakfast table
        is down the stairs,
        thru the hall,
    and there you are.
It's easiest,
    it's closest—
you just keep bearing right
    and lean your way in.

The other morning Peg called;
    I was first to come down to eat.
    Bobby, Mike, Leigh followed.
On impulse I stood up on Leigh's
    high chair in the corner—
    ready to surprise them
    as they came through the hall.
I heard them thunder down the steps—
    my muscles tensed for the pounce.
Then, for a reason unknown to me,
    they made a hard left turn
and I had been flanked.
But I was up there
    so I just stayed
        trying to look as if
    I were waiting for a trolley—
    or something sensible.

Bobby and Mike, eleven & eight,
    sophisticated men of the world,
        ignored me completely.
But two-year-old Leigh
        smiled and said,
    "Hi, Dad. Whatcha doing?"
Now it's not too easy to explain
    why at 7:20 A.M.
        you—a responsible adult—
        are standing of all places
        in a high chair.
"Leigh, I'm waiting up here
    to jump on you—
    lie down—here I come—
    right in the middle
        of your little tummy."
Quick as a flash
    she was down on the floor.
In another instant I sat beside her
    rejoicing in this tribute
of confidence—devotion—
        trust—in one of her
        dad's plans for the moment.

Later on I thought—
        O Lord, help me
    to love You so much,
    to trust You so completely
that if You said lie down, boy
    I'm going to run over you,
        I too would obey
        instantly—completely.

May the quality
        of my devotion
    and the depth
        of my confidence
make Thy great heart glad.

29

Paternal Instinct

"Tom," I said—
  as I looked down at him,
"You can't say a word—
    or play a game,
      or put on your shirt,
    or fix your supper.
You don't have a car
    or a job,
    or go to school—
and besides you're expensive.
The price of babies
  seems to be steadily rising—
  since '52—Bobby
    '56—Michael
    '61—Leigh—
you'd think I'd get some discount.
    And, Tom, you're time consuming—
you won't eat what the rest
    of us do—or when, either.
There you are—my new son—
  just a helpless, broke,
    expensive, noisy
bundle of humanity.
But you can be—
  a happy baby,
    an active boy,
    an exuberant teenager,
    a useful man,
if someone will take the time to—
    feed you,
      clothe you,
        guide you,
          teach you,
        paddle you,
      love you,
    train you—
for you are also one of life's
    choice opportunities—
  a rich and challenging way
    in which to serve God.

If I fail you, there is no way
for me to be a real success.
But if I train you well—
in wisdom,
in faith,
in courage,
in honesty—
I will have risen above
all other failures.
With these great odds at stake
my heart is made to pray—

"O Thou who through
Thy miracle of life
hast bestowed this honor on me,
grant me one more request—
give me Thy grace,
Thy understanding
Thy love—
make me a father—
like Thee.

Shadow

From the time little boys are born
   until they are three or so
they belong to their moms
   but the next three years
belong to their dad.
   I have one of those
three plus-ers at my house.

If I wear a shirt,
   he wears a shirt,
if I go barefooted,
   he goes barefooted,
if I read—he reads,
   if I dig—he digs.
He doesn't ask to go fishing
   or to the park
   or swimming—
it seems enough for him
   just to be with me.
I look forward to the
   weekends with delight
because he will not be more
   than three steps behind me.

When life beats me down a bit
   and I lose the confidence
      to lead,
         to master,
            to choose,
      I sometimes come home
   and just walk around the yard
with Tom a step or two behind.
   Somehow just to feel
      his trust,
         his confidence,
      his devotion,
gives me strength
   to try some more.
You can't fool a little boy
   about character
   and I just accept
his judgment that
   there must be something
to me after all.

Prejudice

Everybody says our newest son
    Patrick Copeland Benson
is a strikingly beautiful baby.
    I readily agree but then
I do have a question
    about my judgement
because I thought all our
    children were beautiful babies.
I felt that Bobby—our first-born
    was the handsomest thing
I had ever seen anywhere.
But fourteen years later as I
    look at snapshots of his tiny face
I either had a very cheap camera
    or he was just barely average.
But at the time—
    as a proud new father
I saw him with eyes
    so completely prejudiced
    and blinded by love
it was pure delight to look at him.

And brings no end
of consolation
    and strength to my heart
to remember when the Heavenly Father
    looks at me, He doesn't see
    the modest victories
        resounding defeats
    courageous aspirations,
        faltering results,
    noble motives,
        shabby attitudes,
    optimistic starts
            and discouraging stops
that are so much a part of me—
        but He looks through eyes of love
and in His sight
        I am transformed
    to a useful, worthy,
            noble being.

Second Helpings

His prayers are not always the same—
    some nights he prays—
"Now I lay me down to sleep . . ."
    simple words, but words
of dignity from his young heart.
    Other nights he begins,
"Our Father which art in heaven . . ."
    and he perfectly repeats—
those beautiful life-giving words.
    But the nights I like best
are the nights he extemporizes and
    this was one of those choice nights.
As a parent your heart leaps—
        from laughter,
            to tears—
        and back again.
"Lord," he prayed, "Give us this day"—
    stymied momentarily he paused—
then in a flash of insight he resumed,
    "Lord, give us some other days too."

Later on I found myself echoing
   this bit of seven-year-old wisdom,
"Give me some tomorrows too, Lord."
   But at our house we have a rule—
which now marched erect past me—
   no extras,
   no "mores",
      no "seconds"—
until the "firsts" are gone.
   No more bacon until
      you've downed the egg—
   no more steak until
      you eat the spinach.
And now this rule that I had made
   for them thrust itself on me.
Do I deserve another day—
   another set of blessings—
   is today's plate clean?
Twenty-four hours,
   fourteen hundred forty minutes,
eighty-six thousand four hundred seconds—
   all mine
      to use,
         to abuse,
      to account for.

"Oh, Lord, help me to take today.
May I with dedication
   use its opportunities,
      accept the reverses,
   share its burdens.
May I be—
   thankful for its graces,
      humble in its successes,
   devoted to its Giver.
May I in some measure—   earn tomorrow—
   by the way I live today."

Obligation

When I was a little boy
   there was a time or two
I thought I had taken
   all an eight year old
   should have to take—
baths, yard mowing,
   trash hauling, orders,
   Sunday school,
piano lessons and
   babysitting with sisters.

The only thing that kept
    me from running away
    was the fact that Mom wouldn't
    let me cross the street.
But I resolved to get a job,
    or rather a position,
and pay them back for everything
    they had ever done for me—
        meals, bicycles,
    swimming suits,
        ball caps, shoes,
    skates, rent—
everything—and then maybe they
    would let me run my own life.
But even then I sorta wondered
    how I'd put a price
    on bedside vigils,
        kisses and bandaids
    for skinned knees and elbows,
        for puzzles, games,
    bedtime stories, ice cream cones,
        love, concern, worry, tears,
    crackling fires in the winter,
        fans in the summer,
    and all the other things so
plainly above and beyond
    the call of parental duty.
Almost daily I still find some
        hidden attitude, habit,
    or value that comes to me
        because of a good name given
and I am made to realize
    an ever deepening obligation
to share a heritage
    with those who call me Dad.

II

THE PASSING SCENE

The Passing Scene

It was a beautiful neighborhood—
  close to town,
    brick sidewalks,
  on the new street car line.
The two-storied homes were new,
  neatly trimmed and kept.
Its streets sang out with sounds
  of boys and girls
    and clothesline conversations.
It was a happy place to live and be.

Sixty-odd years sped quickly by—
  and wider streets,
    expanding population,
  autos, trucks, and buses
pushed the city farther and farther,
  and the once fine neighborhood
slowly became an unsightly mixture
  of light industry,
    empty stores,
  low rent apartments, and
    rundown houses.
Bulldozers, wreckers, and cranes
  finally announced it had become

a project number in an urban renewal plan.
It's sad to see
the once-proud homes destroyed—
homes that knew the ritual of living,
   the happiness of newly-weds,
      the gurgling of babies,
   the patter of little feet,
      the anxiety of sickness,
   the stillness of death—
homes that saw a host
      of happy Christmases,
   and games of hide-and-seek—
homes that sheltered
   from the winds of winter,
      from the rains of spring,
   from the heat of summer—
homes that so nobly served
   now finally condemned
   to bull-dozers,
   wrecking crews,
   and hungry flames.
Scars on the landscape
   speaking silently that
   the things men do—
holding senate seats,
   designing rockets,
      building bridges—
they are here today
      and gone tomorrow.

O Thou who dost not change,
   whose works are everlasting—
Thou whose touch can give—
   a forty-year ministry
      or a cup of cold water
the granite quality of
   the Eternal—
Make the things I do
   worthy of Thy hand
      of permanence.

A Grand Old Lady

I guess about the first place
    my parents ever took me
        was to see her.
She was poorer in those days—
she lived in an older house
    with dark, narrow stairs,
        one room "departments,"
            hand fans and hissing radiators.
She was always a worker though.
    Her years were
        filled with her service,
    her house was
        worn with constant use,
    her heart was
        extended to the needy.
She was someway tied
    into most of my life—
        in the great moments—
            conversion,
        baptism,
            marriage—
    and in the daily round—
        friendship,
        service,
        worship—
she was always right there.
She's labored long and hard,
    deserves ease and contentment.
But with characteristic sacrifice
    and vision she has
        gone in debt again,
            enlarged her house,
            bought new furniture—

just to be ready to serve
my children as she served me.
What a thrill to see her
  with the dignity of age,
    and the energy of youth,
rolling up her sleeves to serve
  a new generation's needs
    in a larger, better way.
Yes, my first trip was to see her,
  and someday I'll go there last—
      first—
          last—
and all the way along life's journey.
  She's been my friend—
    "She's a grand old lady."

Duty's Dignity

Her name was Cissy.
She was solid black,
    and even though there
        was some question
        as to her family tree
she was a fine little dog.
As a pup she had destroyed
    the required number
        of newspapers,
            shoes, and
                flower beds
To reach her maturity.

She had a fine litter of pups,
    seven to be exact
and it was something to watch
    her care for them.
Who taught that little dog,
    so recently a pup herself,
    to care and feed,
        clean and protect
those seven wiggling,
    squirming, yapping
appetites rolled in fur?
Who placed that look of
    intense pride,
        beaming happiness?
Who gave that air of dignity?
    God did.
God made that little dog.
And in His world He gave her
    a share,
        a place to fill,
            a task to perform—
A duty that dignified.

All of God's creatures
   have dignity
but it is only reached through
   the doorway of duty.
He made you to
      stand tall,
   walk straight,
      play fairly,
   love wholeheartedly—
and everytime you
   think the mean thought,
   do the "small" thing
you stoop beneath your dignity.

**Oh God, make us to be
   too tall to be stooped,
   too straight to be crooked,
   too big to be small.
Help us to do
   the tasks that ennoble,
   the duties that dignify.**

Contrast

On one side lay the hills—
   God's hills—
  green and verdant,
   quilted with trees,
  bordered by a brook.
On the other lay the road—
   man's road—
  littered with cans and trash
   weedy and winding,
  guarded by Joe's Beanery signs.
Side by side they stood—a contrast—
  between God's creation—
   of order,
    of beauty,
     of purpose,
and man's works—
  unkept,
   disfigured,
   and so soon outdated.
The house was carefully placed—
  the swing,
   the rockers,
  the windows,
all took aim,
  alas, upon the road.
It seemed to me—
  a shame,
   a mistake,
   almost a crime—

to live in the hills
  and look at the road.
Our generation—
  strangely afflicted,
  inwardly suffering—
from a disease that shows itself—
  in shriveled souls,
    in shallow thoughts,
  in spiritual myopia.
Maybe this is the proper diagnosis—
  too many lives face the road,
  too few "look to the hills".
The hills—hills that can
  put us into perspective,
hills that should inspire us to pray . . .

O Lord, make us
  serene like the hills,
    clear like the sky,
  pure like the clouds,
    upright like the trees,
  warm like the sunshine,
    refreshing like the rain,
  bubbling like the stream.
O Thou Who makest all things—
  and maketh them beautiful—
make us beautiful too.

Hearts And Treasures

Spring is here—
  the young are
    smitten with love,
  the ground is
    covered with greenery,
  and the garage is
    bursting with junk.
Where did it all come from—
  and where is it all going?

With the advent of cleaning time,
    attics everywhere
are "crowdedly testifying"
    that as human beings we are
      accumulators,
        colléctors,
      junk dealers.
And our assortment of goods—
    whether it be
    hats, houses,
    clothes, cameras,
    furniture, lamps—
the Master called our treasure.

He didn't call it treasure
     because of its usefulness—
  lovely chairs—
     minus one leg,
  lots of jars—
     without any tops,
  magazines old enough
     to be in a barber shop.
And not because of its value
  did He call it treasure.
They'd charge you to haul it off.

But treasure, He said,
  because they are
     pictures of places
        where you put
           your heart for awhile.

They were all things
     you could not do without,
  that you just had to have.
Remember—
  the day you signed the notes—
     the painful monthly payments
  to buy this collection
  of things you no longer use.
They were treasures then,
  but just like He said—
     moths and time,
     rust and kids,
        thieves and the dog
have reduced them
  to spring cleaning projects.
Basements, attics, carports—
  eloquently echoing
  the timeless words of
     the Master:
"Be careful what you treasure—
  for where your treasure is
     your heart will be."

51

Christmas Story

I stopped for the light—
  glancing down, I saw
a poor, broken bird on the curb
    in the pose of death.
Waiting for the signal to change
  I fell to talking to him.
What happened little friend?
  Did your radar go out
    or your landing gear fail?
What malfunction sent you falling?
  Did a little boy
with rock, sling, and keen aim
    bring you crashing down?
Or with winter's cold all about,
    was it that you couldn't find food?
What brings you to such an end
  when you were made to soar?

Then as I listened
    he told me the Christmas story.
Oh, he wasn't wearing
    red or green
  or singing carols
    loud and clear—
He didn't speak of Santa Claus
    or of decorating the tree—
he had no tinsel
    or colored lights,
but he seemed to know
    a lot about Christmas—
More than all these other things
    had ever told me.

What does a bird know about
    the story of Christmas?
Christmas is a love story—
  love that sees,
    love that knows,
  love that cares,
and it isn't far from love
    that sees a sparrow fall
to love that sends His Son.

And what is Christmas but
    the supreme expression
    of God's concern and care,
For every step from the manger
    led to Calvary's hill.
Every day the Master lived
    He seemed to say to all,
    "I love you still."
The horn behind said
    the light had changed
and I started to pull away—
    with a grateful heart
to a poor, broken bird
    for the story of Christmas
    he told me that day.

Disparity

I started to pull them up
    and throw them away—
the brown, lifeless remains
    of the twelve shrubs.
I had planted them with pride
    and expectation.
Now they were slain
  by our severest winter
  of the century.

But like most things I do—
    I put it off
and March brought some
    bright sunshine,
      spring rain,
    a few warm nights
and somehow, unbeknownst to me,
    life—wondrous—
    mysterious—thrilling—
burst out of those brown stems
    until they, like all the world—
the trees, grass, buttercups—
    seemed to be saying
in spring's glorious message—
    I love to live!

Men too have this ingrained
     love for life,
          a desire to remain,
     a dread of dying.
History is filled with stories
     of men and women
with nothing left to live for—
     posessions,
          health,
               friends,
          family,
          future all gone—
but they clung to life,
     dearly, grimly,
they tied one more knot
     in the end of the rope.
It runs deep, this desire
     for self-preservation,
          this dread of being snuffed out.

Then how do you explain
     a young man—
          just thirty-three
               in the prime of life
setting His face
     toward Jerusalem
          to die.
The birds were happily warbling
     their songs of spring,
but He walked
     serenely,
          resolutely,
               triumphantly,
to a cross and death—
     cruel,
          agonizing,
               undeserved death.

"Herein is love . . .
     not that we loved Him . . .
But that He loved us . . .
     the recompense for our sins."

55

III

OPENHANDEDNESS

Openhandedness

There is something about fall—
   the turning trees,
    the crisp nights,
   the clear mornings,
    the football games,
   the chrysanthemums—
that makes me feel I like her
   best of all the seasons.
At least I always think so
   after a long hot summer.
And yet with all her beauty—
   trees, flowers,
   and her sweet relief
    from heat, grass cutting—
she arouses in my heart
   a faint sadness, a poignancy.
As the year heads down the stretch
   and the days grow shorter,
   she seems to quietly say
    "There's a time to plant,
     a time to grow,
    and a time for winter's blast."

I learned this feeling early—
    this sense of "mortalness."
When I was a boy there was no joy
   quite like that which a
    sunny Saturday morning brought—
there was fishing and games
   and swimming and
  cowboys and Indians
and mud between your toes.
But the hours raced by
   and in my childish heart I knew
there was a time to play,
   to swim, to run, to laugh,
but the darkness was coming
   and the bath tub waited,
and I felt an inner pain because
   I could not halt the day.

And I know it now—I look
   at Bob, Mike, Leigh, Tom, Pat—
seated around my table
   and my heart wells up
  with pride, joy, happiness,
marred only by this faint pang,
   that moments I'd clutch to myself
   are so swiftly passing by.
Oh to be able to release
   these moments into His Hand—
gladly, unbegrudgingly, freely
   like a tree sheds its leaves—
happy, secure, in this certainty—
that in His plan
there's always another spring.

Life Is So Daily

Nearly everything I do
  needs doing again so soon—
most everything I did today
  will have to be re-done
  tomorrow or at least
  by the end of the week.
Shaving, eating,
  driving to work,
    cleaning the gutters,
      building the fire,
    answering the mail,
  keeping up with the Joneses,
talking on the phone.
These and a hundred other things
  make up my waking hours
  day after day,
    week after week,
until at times it seems
  most of my life
    is spent in a
  succession of marches
    that do not matter
  and numberless causes
    that do not count.
And I am made to wonder—
  will I give myself away
  bit by bit—
    time, thought
    energy, love
    emotion, will—
to a collection of
  choices and projects
  which will die as I do
  because they mattered
    only to me.

Somehow may I use
  the lumber of my life—
  to build a ladder—
  straight, sturdy, true
  on which men may climb
  until they come to Thee.
Or to fashion a cathedral—
  a quiet, holy place
  where men would pause
  and seek Thy ways.
Or to plant a tree—
  tall, serene, fruitful
  whose shade would someday
  grant a traveler rest.
Let me share in Thy works
  not asking that I must
  see the results in my day,
but laboring in this confidence—
  because it was done in Thee
    it will someday
    come to fulfillment
and I will not have lived
  worthlessly,
    selfishly,
      needlessly.

Multiple Me's

Most of the time it seems there
  is just not enough of me
  to go around.
At the office it is almost as
  if I leave more to do than
  I am ever able to get done.
And when I'm home—the yard,
  the family, the woodpile,
  the garage all seem to have a
  rightful claim on my time.
All of the projects that I would
  like to be able to begin—
  the books I would like to read—
  could all be done if there
  were only more of me to do them.

But then there are times when
  there are just
    too many of me.
One of those times is when I pray.
If only Bob, the sincere, the
  quiet, the desirer of holy
  things could make his way
    alone to the place of prayer
  and make his petitions known,
  and there find the
    power and poise
  his heart must have.
But every time he goes to pray
  a whole multitude of me comes
  trooping right along—
    Bob the impatient,
  Bob the referee heckler,
    Bob the unconcerned,
  and the ambitious Bob
    and the unkind Bob.

And by the time they all crowd
   into the closet,
there is such a din
      and clamor that
   I can hardly hear
      the voice of God.
And then I am made to see
   that what I am—
      in my thoughts
   at work, at play,
      in traffic—
   all these people
make up the person I am
   when I kneel down to pray.
Oh, that I would love Him so
   dearly that every moment
   of my life—
   ease, thought, pain,
   pleasure, toil, dreams—
would be but a preparation
   for those times when
   I shall be alone
      with Him.

Practicing The Presence

A great composer hears music
   and writes it down
      that others may hear it too.
A great artist sees beauty
   and puts it on a canvas
      that others may enjoy it also.
And a devout Christian feels a Presence,
   and lives his life like he's not alone
      that others may know Him too.

People often pray—
   "We beseech thee to come"
When the real prayer should be—
   "Thou art here—
      Help me to sense it."

The simple truth is—
   as a dimpled baby,
      a mischievous child,
      a perplexed teenager,
      a harried adult—
you never leave
      the presence of God
   for He is always near.
The problem is to know it.
Like inspiration to
   the musician,
      the artist—
these times of awareness,
   spiritual perception,
seem to come and go in one's life.
And at times I am swept away in
   the grace of communion,
      the posture of praise—
times of almost
   inexpressible joy,
      overwhelming fellowship,
   uncontrollable song.

They come—
    not as often as I'd like,
    not everytime I wish it so—
but they come unannounced like
    the calling winds,
        the refreshing showers.
Then suddenly they're gone
    and I am "me" again.
"Me",
    with a family to feed,
    with a living to make.
But somehow "me"—
    a little stronger,
    a little better,
for having been with Him.
But I cannot help but wonder
    What kind of person
        I could be if
daily—
    hourly—
        or "alway-ly"—
I could learn
    to walk with Him.

Synopsis

To look at me—
   138 pounds of pure dynamite—
you'd never know
   I used to be sickly.
But it's true—I had them all—
   scarlet fever, flu,
      mumps, measles, hives,
      pneumonia, asthma and
   and a hundred others.
It seemed to me I was
      the first to catch it,
   the last to let it go.
During those days of quiet
   I learned to love to read.

As a boy I
   sailed the high seas,
      braved raging storms,
   hacked through jungles,
      explored dark Caves,
in hot pursuit of—
   "The Hardy Boys"
   "Tom Sawyer"
   "Robinson Crusoe"
   "Nancy Drew"
and other assorted heroes.
   They always
caught the villain,
   rescued the baby,
      won the battle,
   found the money and
lived happily ever afterwards.

   As I grew older
I began to read books in which
   the hero died
      or the wrong guy married
   the fair young princess.

You know the kind—
books with true-to-life endings.
   I guess I'm sentimental,
      even childish,
but I like books that end well.
Let the hero be
   down and nearly out,
      shot and left for dead—
but let him win in the end.

And so I like the Bible
   because it ends well.
It begins with the heroes
   in a sinless, deathless land—
but they tripped, fell—
   and began
a downward journey that led
      through misery,
   failure, sorrow,
      and shame—
until finally you say,
   they'll never make it back.
But when it ends,
   they're home again—
it took God's Son to do it—
      but it ends well.

In these days with the world
   divided into two camps—
      glaring back and forth
like two little boys
   across a line in the dust,
with hatred, strife,
      wars and rumors—
   it's nice to know that
the One who started it well
      will also see that it ends
   according to His plan.

He Had It Coming

He promised he would
    but he didn't;
He'd said he could
    but he hadn't;
He'd let me down,
    put me off,
he had it coming—
    so I gave it to him—
skillfully, enthusiastically,
    I let him have it.
And then a part of me
the part that's made of earth
    said at'ta boy,
    that's telling him,
    that'll get him moving—
that's the old business drive—
    plenty of push—hustle—
you sure showed him.
    And then another part of me
a part that's made like God
    whispered soft and clear
"You showed him all right—
    you showed him everything—
everything, that is, but
    forbearance
        kindness
            forgiveness
                longsuffering—
in short, everything—but
    Christlikeness."
    But he had it coming,
        he got what he deserved,
the earth was quick to say.

But remember Christ, the image replied.
   You failed Him,
     broke your promises.
   You missed the mark,
  you deserved judgment
    but—you needed mercy—
He gave you what you needed
    instead of what you deserved.
Now the struggle ceased—both voices
    bowed in prayer . . .

**Oh God—make me sensitive
  not to what people deserve—
     but rather to their needs—
  make me like Christ.**

Erosion

He was a college student—
   he seemed so sure,
   he was so positive,
   he just missed cockiness.
   I thought in college
I knew all the answers too
   but it seems that someone
has thought up some new questions.
    The older you get—
   the more inclined you are
   to see the risks,
   to raise objections,
    to vote against it.
Hastily we say this is
   our superior judgment,
   that impetuous youth is gone.
But sometimes isn't it really faith
   weakened and corroded
   by your failures,
   your ill fated ventures,
   and your lost battles.
The Master talked of
   "the faith of a little child."
There has been a time when each
   of my children thought
    I could
   fix anything,
    lick anybody,
   answer any questions,
    win any race—
(ideas that were doomed
    to be short lived).

But maybe that's what Christ meant—
    God wants you to believe
        that He can,
            that He has the power.
    Sure you've failed—
        but He hasn't,
    sure you've retreated—
        but He didn't,
    sure you're weak—
        but He isn't.
He wants you to believe
    with the buoyant,
        optimistic,
            bright-eyed
                expectant,
faith of a little child rather
    than the defeated,
        pessimistic,
            "burned-once"
                gloomy,
            faith of an adult.

A Sweet Gum Tree

It was a lovely summer morning—
  the sky was blue,
    the sun shining,
  the breezes blowing.
It had been a hard week
  replete with details,
    frustrations and
  late evening work.
But this day I couldn't get
  moving—I was
  tired, nervous,
  just plain beat.
I made several starts at work
  but kept ending up
  on the front porch,
  piled on the lounge.
Lying there, I looked at the
  wind blow through
  the treetops.

Close by the front porch
   stands a sweet gum tree.
It looks as if at one time
   something nearly killed it
   until now it is a strange
   combination of the lovely
   and the grotesque.
A part of the tree is alive—
   drinking in the rain,
   reaching for the sunshine,
     playing in the breezes.
And part of it is dead—
   unmoved, unfeeling,
   untouched by the wonderful
   graces of God.

A sweet gum tree
   quietly showing me the way—
     the way I was
   in stark contrast
     to the way that
   God through His Spirit
     meant me to be.
A sweet gum tree
   causing me
   to breathe this prayer—

So fill me with Thy life
   that I shall—
feel Thy slightest touch,
   hear Thy softest whisper,
see Thy faintest footprint—
yielding in such glad response
   that others might see
     the grace and beauty
   of communion with Thee.

Digging

God and I raised a flower bed—
  He really did the most
I guess because we used
    His soil,
      His air,
    His water,
      His life,
    His sun.
My part seemed so trivial that
  I said, "Lord—
    you take those bulbs and
    make them grow
    right here in the box
    out in the garage—
you don't need me, Lord,
    you can do it by Yourself."
    "No," He said—
  I want to do My part,
  I'm waiting to begin,
but you must do yours, too.
  You'll have to
    dig the bed,
      bury the bulbs,
    pull the weeds."
"Okay," I said, and
    I did my feeble part
and God took those bulbs—
    burst them with life,
  fed them with soil,
    showered them with rain,
  drew them with sunshine
until we had beautiful flowers.

And then He seemed to say,
  "Your life is like a garden
and if you'd like, we'll make it
  a beautiful thing.
I'll furnish
  the soil of grace,
    the sunshine of love,
  the rains of blessing,
    the wonder of life,
But you must do the digging."

"Lord, you just go ahead—
Make me what You want me to be—
    make me a saint,
  fill me with compassion,
    give me great faith."
"No", He said, "You've got to
  keep your heart tilled,
    hoe the weeds of evil,
    chop away the second-best.
I'll make you anything—
    pure,
      clean,
        noble,
          useful—
anything you want to be—
  but only if you dig."

IV

TO AN UNKNOWN PICKET

To An Unknown Picket

He was just a lone picket,
the representative of his local—
    a silent, sign-bearing,
rather good-natured, reliable,
    laborer turned picket.
He was there to protest
    some difference between
    his union and the contractor
    putting up a large new building
    across the street and up the hill,
    a door or two from us.

Three old buildings were razed,
    completely demolished.
He enthusiastically waved his sign
    to pedestrians, workmen,
    deliverymen, sidewalk
        superintendents;
everybody had to look at his sign.
A gigantic hole was excavated—
he just kept walking and waving.
    They poured the floors
        first,
            second,
        third,
            fourth.
Dump trucks, bulldozers, cranes,
    jackhammers, concrete mixers,
and all that he had
        was a sign and a helmet
    but he kept right on waving.
The building was nearly completed—
    lovely marble exterior,
    ornamental concrete trim—
a sort of monument
    to my friend's failure—
it looks like they'll make it
    in spite of all he can do.
But he's undismayed, undaunted,
    I saw him today waving his sign.

I don't know whether his local
    was underpaid—overworked,
    or overpaid—underworked,
        who was in the right
        or in the wrong.
But either way, I think this fellow
    should be Picket of the Year.
The rains of spring,
    the snows of winter,
        the heat of summer,
the embarrassment of failure—
    nothing seems to dishearten
        this mighty warrior
        of the picket line.

Somehow every time I see him
    I breathe this silent prayer:
O God, as I work for Thee
    When I seem to fail—
may I try again.
    When the odds are long—
may I still press on.
    When You give me a task—
may I see it through.
        Somehow, some way,
    make me faithful, too.

The Misfit

It seemed to be his lot—
   he was one of those
unfortunate people with a talent to be
   always in the wrong place,
     always at the wrong time.
He was born wrong—
   the declining Roman empire,
     the broken home,
   the conquered Jewish nation,
     the poverty-stricken slums.
He lived wrong—
    others went to school—
   he played hookey,
    others played ball—
   he stole apples,
    others learned trades—
   he learned to cheat.
Just a common thief—
   he started wrong,
  he lived wrong,
   and it looked as if
     he'd finish wrong.
The wrong place
     and the wrong time—
  a Roman cross,
   a painful death,
  a final shame.

When from the middle cross
   came words of redeeming love,
"You shall be with Me in paradise."
   In all the stream of history
   one and only one of
   the numberless sons of Adam
could have said those words—
   and he hung beside Him.
   What tremendous fortune—
   what wondrous providence—
in one instant, his life—
      given to evil,
   thoroughly misused,
   doomed to die—
was changed and ended
   in crowning glory.
It was the one sentence
   without which
      there is no success.
It was the one sentence
   which redeems all failure,
and it was said to him
   at life's final flickering moment.
   The one most important issue of all
      was gloriously solved—
at long last he was
   in the right place
   at the right time!

The Helper

"Howdy!" he said
  as he stuck out his hand
when he first came into town.
  Kind-faced,
    gentle-spirited,
  open-hearted,
he stayed for awhile,
  and he used those hands
    to fix wagons,
      mend fences,
        lift burdens,
and in dozens of ways
  he helped folks out.
It wasn't too long until
    everybody in town
had been touched and helped
  by those kind, strong hands.

But one day a crowd of folks,
    even me, I'm sorry to say,
in a fit of temper,
    on a trumped-up charge,
stretched his arms out
    as wide as they would go
    against a cruel wooden cross
and drove spikes clear through
        those strong
            helpful hands.

When it was done and our anger
    had cooled to reason again
we knew we had done him wrong.
        We thought for sure
he'd leave us now
        as soon as he'd gotten even.
But he came right back,
        and to our surprise—
    with that same "howdy",
    and outstretched hand
he quietly took his place
    healing,
        blessing,
            helping.

        Those strong hands—
    they didn't have to help at all;
        those gentle hands—
    they never did an unkind thing;
        those pierced hands—
    they were punished so cruelly;
        those loving hands—
His hands—
        God's hands—
    twice reached out to man.

Impetus

It was all over now—
with Him gone
there was no use
trying to go on.
For it was built around Him—
His words,
His authority,
His deeds.
He was the attraction.
If He were only sick,
someday He'd be well;
if He'd only been imprisoned,
someday He would be released
and they would start over;
the cause could be resumed.

But He was dead—
irrevocably,
finally,
unchangeably
gone.
They were sorry it was over
but sadly sure it was.
They would always be glad
they'd come—even though
it hadn't worked out.
They could never forget
the Master—
His countenance
His thoughts
His compassion—

These had been great days
and now they were past.
Discouraged now—defeated—
just plain afraid—
when they could face it,
they were going back—
back to Galilee
back to tax tables
and to fish nets—
away from this crowded city
with its high priest,
its temple guards,
jeering mobs,
Roman soldiers
and cruel crosses.

Then it happened—
the impossible,
the unbelievable,
the only thing
in all the world that would
bring them back—
the only thing
that would fill them with
a bravery that defied death—
the only thing
that could send the cause
streaming forth again
with a now unconquerable
force.
He had risen from the dead,
He was alive again.

Residue

It was about all
    he had left.
He started out
    richly endowed with
      great abilities,
    rising prominence
    and driving energy.
But he'd largely wasted it all
    ministering to small groups
    or uneducated heathen,
      unimportant people,
    unfortunate slaves.

Slowly it had passed—
    preached, beaten,
    walked and washed away.
For he'd paid a price
    to preach the cross—
  his promising future
    his increasing importance
  his place of prominence—
he traded them all
    for a rugged life of
    shipwrecks, dusty roads,
    failures, and stormy seas.
He'd lost his youth,
    expended his strength,
    surrendered his standing.
But through it all
    he was able to say
"I have kept the faith."

It was nearly over now—
   a Roman court,
   an axman's blade,
   and a martyr's death
would prove he had chosen well.
He'd traded the things
   he could not keep
for the treasure
   he could not lose.

And with a similar generous hand
   life makes her gifts to you
      a span of time,
      a portion of strength,
   a quiver of talents—
but sooner or later
   she comes again
   and asks for them—
      one by one—
and when she's taken them
   all away—make sure,
      like Paul—
   your faith remains.

Tax Collector

It was going to be another scorcher—
  Levi dreaded to go to work.
The pay was good but
  the job was distasteful.
The Jews, his own people,
  hated him,
  glared at him,
  called him names.
The Romans, his employers
  treated him like dirt.
Dreading another day—
  the insults of the Jews,
    the sneers of the Romans,
  the hot burning sun.
He plodded toward the market place.
  Levi—whose name
    meant "joined to"
hardly seemed to belong anywhere.

Looking up from his table he saw
   five men passing by.
Three of them looked the other way,
   one looked at him with disdain
but the one who walked in front,
   young, earnest, erect,
looked at him—like no one had
   since he'd been a little boy.
His countenance, his bearing,
   his attitude, his eyes—
all seemed to say—
   "I like you—
I wish you'd go with me."

He was used to jeers—
   he jeered right back;
he was used to curses—
   he swore right back
but he couldn't withstand
   this attack of concern
and he found himself in step
   with this one who seemed to care.
The Jews saw a traitor,
   the Romans saw a collaborator,
But Jesus saw a poor lonely man
   who needed a friend.

There are lots of people like Levi—
   people who could
      sing a song,
   write a poem—
but it's locked up deep inside
   waiting to be released.
You can bring out the worst in folk—
   or be a key that unlocks
      the best—

To Reba

Let others wish you money,
　　Cadillacs, big houses
　　　French poodles, rings
　　and widespread fame—
no doubt they're on their way.
　　This album, your first
says that all these things
　　　will soon be yours,
You and your easy, graceful way
　　reveal a song's deep meanings.
It is so thoroughly enjoyable
　　and deeply inspirational
that all of the assorted symbols
　　of success can hardly
help but be a step away.
　　But let others wish you money—
I'd wish for you the ability
　　to sing all the songs
　　　you ever record
with the fresh faith
　　of a teenager,
with the deep compassion,
　　and with the high ideals
that are so much
　　　a part of you
　　and the way you sing.

For these things,
   humility,
      faith,
         grace,
things that so richly comprise
   the talent with which
      you now sing
are so very often
   the very first things
success steals from
      those who succeed.
Let others wish you money—
   I'd like to wish for you
      riches instead.